Otto von Frisch

Hamsters

**How to Take Care of Them
and Understand Them**

With color photographs by Karin Skogstad
and drawings by György Jankovics

Consulting Editor: Matthew M. Vriends, Ph.D.

BARRON'S

Contents

however, make sure it is too heavy to be tipped over (made of earthenware or porcelain) and easy to clean.

A water bottle: Water is best provided through an upside-down water bottle that can be fastened to the cage bars or attached to the glass of the terrarium by means of rubber suction cups. The bottle should have a valve to keep water from dripping into the cage. Hamsters learn instantly how to use such a device.

Giving water in a bowl is not recommended because hamsters quickly kick bedding and food into it.

Things to Play with and Gnaw on

With their plump little bellies and cheeks stuffed full of food, hamsters are hardly the image of athletic energy. Their appearance doesn't give any indication of their love of exercise. The horizontal bars of the cage offer some

No matter what you offer your hamster, it will immediately explore how the object can be used for climbing. Here a brick is being used for daring acrobatics.

climbing fun, but they become old hat and get boring after a while. Your hamster will therefore be grateful for additional climbing opportunities and some new challenges now and then. Give free rein to your imagination when outfitting your hamster's cage.

Natural twigs with rough bark: Wooden branches and twigs are used by hamsters for climbing and sharpening claws as well as to satisfy the need for gnawing. Cut away forks that form an angle that is too narrow, for your hamster might get a foot caught in the crook if it is too tight. You can squeeze the branches between the bars of the cage or tie them in place with raffia. But be sure to check them routinely for stability.

Important: Use only branches from nonpoisonous trees. Fruit tree branches are ideal if you are absolutely sure that they have not been sprayed. If you have the slightest doubt, take branches from other trees, such as oak, alder, elderberry, chestnut, basswood, poplar, or willow. Even here you have to exercise caution: Don't gather branches along the roadside, for trees growing there are exposed to exhaust fumes from cars, and toxic substances are absorbed by the wood. Even if you collect branches in parks and woods, they should be hosed down well with hot water and allowed to dry before being placed in the cage. Unfortunately, harmful substances penetrate even to supposedly safe places.

Wooden ladders: These can be used to provide access to raised sleeping houses or as bridges placed across branches.

Other accessories: Pet stores also sell seesaws and small merry-go-rounds, but these things are meant to be used outside the cage. Inside, they take up too much room.

Not recommended for hamsters are things made of plastic. This smooth material offers no hold to a hamster's

Walking on a seesaw can also keep a hamster trim and occupied. This item should be set up in the room during the periods for running free. In the cage it would take up too much room.

This climbing excursion is starting out with a "rope climb."

The first branch is almost conquered.

feet, and your pet could easily slip and get hurt falling. In addition, gnawing may produce plastic splinters that can cause internal injuries if swallowed.

Some Remarks about Exercise Wheels

The famous exercise wheels, or treadmills, designed for small animals have advantages as well as disadvantages for hamsters. On the one hand they are a source of plentiful exercise. But hamsters sometimes become practically addicted to the devices, and running in an exercise wheel is an extremely one-sided form of exercise. If your hamster should be the kind that runs itself ragged every night in its treadmill, you may find it getting on your nerves because the wheels tend to begin squeaking and rattling noisily after prolonged use.

If your hamster's cage is large enough and contains plenty of equipment for acrobatics, I would advise you to do without an exercise wheel. For once a hamster has gotten hooked on the device, taking it away leaves the animal frustrated and it may become aggressive or apathetic and depressed as a result.

Finally, Three Extras

So far I have discussed only things necessary to a hamster's well-being that are commonly available. If you wish to offer your hamster something different, here are a few ideas.

A toy you can make yourself: On page 13 you will find a picture of a kind of merry-go-round that most hamsters take to enthusiastically and that you can easily make yourself. You will need a round piece of wood about 1 inch thick (2–2.5 cm), a block of wood about $2 \times 2 \times 5$ inches ($5 \times 5 \times 12$ cm), a thin

Accomplished! Time out for a short rest stop.

Now a slow descent. The solid ground is not far off.

metal tube, and a metal bolt that fits into the tube. Set the metal tube into the wooden block at a slight tilt. Then stick the bolt through the center of the wooden disk and fasten it with a washer and a nut. Now insert the end of the bolt into the metal tube. The wooden disk will be tilted above the wooden block at a slight angle.

A separate sand box for digging: Hamsters love to dig and burrow. The instinct to build tunnels and caves is still fully alive even in domesticated hamsters. Being able to act out this instinct in a box especially provided for this purpose—that is, in a place separate from the ordinary living quarters—would be hamster heaven. Of course the area and the height of the sand box have to be at least as big as those of the cage. The bigger the box, the better. And it has to be of solid construction, so that no holes are

chewed through it after just a short time.

The best material for filling the box is a thick layer of sterilized soil or litter for small pets (see The Right Kind of Bedding, page 14).

Let your hamster use its sandbox in the evening, during its phase of greatest activity.

Ornamental cork as a building element: All pet-supply stores sell ornamental cork. The cork is really designed for use in aquariums and terrariums, but thanks to the lively imagination of hamsters it can also be incorporated into their cages. Some hamsters like to convert a piece of rounded cork of appropriate size into a "prefab" roof for a nest they have burrowed for themselves. They then sleep hidden under the cork or, if something arouses their interest, peek out from under it with curious eyes.

In the photos:
Hamsters are talented acrobats. For climbing they rely mostly on their strong front paws, with which they can grab for a secure hold. The hind legs are used only to provide support.

17

Learning to Treat a Hamster Properly

Hamsters are full of curiosity. This trait helps them get oriented quickly in a new environment. It will not take your hamster long before it feels quite at home with you.

The Right Location

Before you bring home your hamster you should set up its cage and choose a permanent place for it. There are a few things to keep in mind:

• A hamster needs peace and quiet so that it can sleep undisturbed during the day.

• The ideal temperature for hamsters is 68° to 72° F (20–22° C), that is, normal room temperature. If it gets to below 50° F (10° C), as in an unheated room in winter, hamsters go into hibernation, and they rarely survive temperatures below freezing.

• Hamsters easily catch cold if exposed to drafts. That is why a cage should never be placed on the floor but should, if possible, be kept at table height. Because of the danger of falls, the cage door always has to be closed carefully.

• Sun or too much light does not agree with hamsters. Don't place the cage in the direct sunlight.

• Air that is either too dry or too humid is bad for a hamster's health. Ideally the air humidity should be from 40 to at most 50 percent. That range is also comfortable for human beings.

The New Home

Make every effort to bring your new hamster, packed in its transport box, home as quickly as you can. The unfamiliar situation it finds itself in makes the animal redouble its efforts to free itself. If it manages to chew a hole in the cardboard box, you may suddenly catch sight of your pet hamster scurrying around in the bus or in your car, and if worse comes to worst, you may never retrieve it.

As soon as you arrive at home, place the box with the hamster in the cage, open the box, and wait until the animal decides to emerge. Put some of the old nesting material you have brought from the pet shop into the sleeping house. This material is imbued with the animal's smell and conveys the message: This is my home and my bed even though the surroundings don't look right. To help the animal feel welcome you should offer it some of the food it is used to. That is all you can do for the time being.

Gentle Acclimation

At first most hamsters are rather confused and frightened from the tranport and the many new impressions they have been subjected to. There are, of course, some exceptionally inquisitive individuals that seem to have no problems adjusting. But in most cases it takes about a week before a hamster gets used to its new home.

Ways to help your hamster:

• Cover the cage with a light cloth during the transition period. This gives the hamster a chance to explore its cage thoroughly and without distractions.

• Leave the animal alone except for feeding it and changing its water.

• Don't change anything in the cage at this stage. This will help the hamster feel at home more quickly.

• Tell visitors curious to meet your new pet to be patient and wait until later.

Learning to Feel at Home

The exploratory phase: After a short period during which the animal usually retreats to its sleeping house, the hamster will start investigating its new surroundings through its senses of smell and touch. It will first sniff the air suspiciously, then creep along the cage walls sniffing, and finally crisscross the cage interior. This whole time the whiskers are feeling for things up close. Usually the cage corners are examined with special thoroughness.

Marking: To feel really at home, animals like hamsters, which rely primarily on their olfactory organs, mark their living area with their scent. To do this, hamsters emit a secretion from two glands located on the sides of the body.

Nest building: A nest is usually built during the first night. If you have placed both old and new nesting material in the cage, the hamster will busily transport everything to the building site. Soft material is carried in the cheek pouches, and stiff stalks of straw are picked up with the teeth. The final building style varies with the individual: Some hamsters incorporate all the material the way they find it, others break it down by picking it apart with their front teeth.

Hand-Taming Your Hamster

Because hamsters have been bred for so many generations under human care they are no longer really wild animals. Baby hamsters born in a cage automatically learn to accept the presence and smell of the humans who take care of them and their parents. The hamster you have purchased no doubt knows that people present no threat to it unless its previous owner has treated it roughly. But such cases are an exception.

In spite of their familiarity with humankind, hamsters are quite capable of putting their incisors to effective use

in self-defense if they feel threatened. This can happen if you accidentally frighten them or pick them up when they are not prepared for it. Then all the instincts these plucky little animals need to survive in the wild come into action. It is therefore most important for your new housemate to have a chance to familiarize itself with your hand and its smell.

By offering special treats you can get your hamster used to your hand and its smell quickly.

The best time to play with your hamster is in the evening, when these animals become active. Don't try to rouse your hamster from sleep just because you have some time and would like to play. Even when a hamster wakes up on its own, it first needs some time by itself. It wants to visit its bathroom spot in peace and eat something before it is ready for action. So wait until your hamster has gone through its evening routine before

19

Nibbling on dog biscuits, twigs, and similar hard things helps wear the incisors down. This is important because these teeth keep growing.

Even large hunks of food are broken down in no time at all.

approaching it. But the more regularly you spend time with the animal after it has finished its evening ritual—every day and at the same time—the faster your hamster will get to know and trust you.

The first step: After a "grace period" of a week you can begin to approach your hamster. Simply reach your hand into the cage and keep it there motionless as you talk quietly and wait for the animal to come up and sniff it. Depending on the your hamster's temperament, this can take three or four days.

The second step: Hold out a small treat between your thumb and forefinger (a shelled walnut or a piece of apple). Don't let go of it as soon as the hamster reaches for it with its front paws or its teeth. If you do, the animal will have disappeared back into its house before you know it. If you hold on to the treat, the hamster will start nibbling on it between your fingers.

The third step: While the hamster is eating, you can pet it gently along the side with your free hand. Don't reach toward the body unexpectedly from

The cheek pouches are almost full. In just a moment the provisions will be taken to a safe storage place.

behind or above because that would frighten a hamster that is not yet quite tame.

Important Reminders for Children

- Reach for the hamster gently.
- Respect the animal's resting times (especially during the adjustment period).
- Don't pet it too much or too long at any one time.
- Wash your hands after touching the hamster.

How to Pick up a Hamster

When your hamster has gotten somewhat used to you, you can try to pick it up gently. There are different ways of proceeding:

1st method: Place one hand underneath the animal and the other one on top to make a warm cave shaded from light. Young hamsters especially feel safe and secure this way.

2nd method: Cup your hands together in such a way that the tips of the fingers of the two hands touch and

In the photos:
Hoarding is one of the hamster's most typical traits. These rodents stash everything edible into their cheek pouches to take the food somewhere where it can be consumed in peace and safety.

21

the thumbs are lined up next to each other. This "roof" is then placed over the hamster. As soon as the hamster is thus enclosed in your hands, move your two little fingers close together.

3rd method: Reach for the hamster with one hand, encircling its body between the front and back legs with your thumb and the fingers (see drawing on right). Your grasp has to be secure but not exert any pressure.

4th method: A simple way for people not used to handling hamsters is what I like to call the "container technique." Find a container into which the animal will fit easily (a small cardboard box or an empty coffee can, for instance) and hold it in front of the hamster with one hand. Usually the hamster will quickly enter this interesting cavity, and you can pick it up. This method is the easiest and particularly suitable for an inexperienced caretaker who has agreed to look after the animal while you are away.

It is wrong to pick a hamster up by the scruff of its neck. Only young hamster babies put up with this, and they are, in fact, carried this way by their mother. Fully grown animals usually protest against being treated this way by squirting some urine.

My tip: As long as you are still not quite used to handling a hamster, hold the animal over a table or some other safe landing place so that your pet won't be hurt should you accidentally drop it.

If a Hamster Bites

Hamsters have sharp front teeth shaped like miniature chisels for breaking down their food, which is often hard. In the wild these teeth are also used for defense against enemies. Many a dog has let go of a common hamster that sank its teeth into the canine's lips or ears. The hamster then often succeeded in escaping to its burrow. Your hamster, too, can bite if it

Hamsters love changes of activity. Being petted now and then, eating at a leisurely pace, doing a thorough job of grooming, climbing and running around for a while, and taking a nap every so often—this is how a hamster likes to pass the time.

feels attacked or is scared (see Five Rules for Approaching a Hamster, page 23). It is therefore wise to avoid doing anything that might be frightening or upsetting to the hamster, particularly during the acclimation period. And, please, react with understanding if your

Picking up a hamster requires the right touch. If you squeeze too hard you may hurt the little animal, and if your grip is not firm enough, your pet may slip out of your hand and fall to the ground.

hamster should use its teeth on you in self-defense. Punishment and loud scolding are pointless and would only make the animal, frantic by now, more likely to bite.

Reacting properly: At this point I would like to warn you against reacting the way a friend of mine did once in my presence: When trying to pick up his hamster he grabbed it so awkwardly that the only recourse the animal had was to bite him in the finger. Because of the pain my friend tried to shake off the little beast as quickly as possible. Unintentionally he threw it to the floor with full force. The hamster did not survive. In a similar case I heard about, the hamster survived but broke all four legs. Understandable as such a reaction to sudden pain is, I still strongly urge you, if you ever find yourself in a similar situation, to disengage yourself from your hamster as gently as you can.

Treatment of a bite wound: Squeeze the wound well and apply tincture of iodine or some other disinfecting medication. If the place of the bite keeps hurting or if it swells up, be sure to consult a doctor.

Five Rules for Approaching a Hamster

1. Never wake a hamster from a deep sleep.

2. Never squeeze it too hard, pinch it, or squash it.

3. Leave it alone if it evades your hand, squeals, or makes a muttering sound. This means that it wants to be left in peace.

4. Don't touch the animal if it rolls over on its back and shows its teeth. Hamsters assume this defensive position when they feel threatened.

5. Put on leather gloves to separate two hamsters that are fighting.

Meeting the Hamster's Needs

Like all animals, a hamster needs enough space and freedom to indulge in its natural behavior. It wants to be able to groom itself thoroughly, eat, climb, run, and punctuate these activities with short naps. The more you allow it to follow this innate life rhythm, the happier and healthier it will be.

Play and affection within limits: Don't think you are acting purely in your hamster's interests if you carry it around and pet it all the time. I have to stress here once more that hamsters are not toys. They can react with apathy or irritation to constant distraction, and they can even get sick and die relatively young. Your hamster will, when it has become quite tame, climb up on your hand and let itself be placed in your lap and stroked. But how often it does this should be up to the animal.

Providing for changes in routine: Living in a cage, a hamster is deprived of all the things that would keep it on the go in the wild. There are no predators against which it has to protect itself. Food, which it would have to search for in nature, is always there. The burrow, or nest, is right next to the food supply. There is no new territory to explore. If cage life continued uninterrupted in this uneventful, monotonous fashion, your hamster's behavior would soon deteriorate into apathy and inactivity, and the animal would age before its time. That is why it is important not only to let your hamster move around regularly outside the cage (see page 24) but also to keep the inside of the cage interesting.

Ways to reduce the monotony of cage life:
● Replace items in the cage, such as branches, about once a week. Any new smell provides a welcome change.
● Bring home a few willow or hazelnut branches or twigs from a fruit tree for

An intimidating posture that may move smaller enemies to take to their heels. To make itself appear larger, the hamster rises up on its hind legs and puffs up its cheeks.

Nose pointed heavenward—and keep following it . . . until you can go no farther.

nibbling now and then.
• Put a tube of undyed cardboard—the inside of a roll of toilet paper, for instance—into the cage. Hamsters love crawling through such a "pipe."
• Place a handful of grass or dry leaves in the cage now and then. A multitude of interesting smells will keep your hamster busy for quite a while.
• Set up some split bricks separated by passageways about 1 1/4 inches (3 cm) wide, making sure they can't be knocked over. The hard-to-reach nooks and crannies thus created are reminiscent of the life-saving hiding places that play such an important role in a wild hamster's life and will be of endless fascination to your pet.

Running Free in the Apartment

When your hamster is fully grown (at about six to eight weeks) and when it feels fully at home, no longer fears your hand, and lets itself be picked up without protest, you should let it out of its cage now and then in the evening and allow it to run free in a closed room. Investigating this new territory will rouse all the animal's senses to full alertness. Rugs and wallpaper beckon, promising excellent nesting material. Narrow spaces behind furniture make wonderful burrows to hide and rest. And perhaps there will be a seesaw waiting to provide physical-fitness exercise.

Things to watch out for: An animal as small and as lively and curious as a hamster, is, of course, likely to encounter all kinds of dangers when running free in a room. All too often a hamster gets squashed accidentally by a closing door, is stepped on, or is killed by a flower vase it was trying to explore and knocked over. Accidents of this sort are by no means rare (see

One look down the other side . . .   *and then back home as fast as possible.*

Dangers for Hamsters, page 27). All I can do is to impress on you the importance of keeping a careful eye on your pet when you let it run free.

Quite apart from the hazards to their own health and well-being, hamsters can also do considerable mischief. One of my hamsters once disappeared unnoticed into a laundry basket. When I found it again the next day, it had already managed to ruin three shirts, five pairs of underpants, and a pair of stockings, and I had quite a time defending the culprit against my mother. Hamster teeth endanger not just laundry but things like newspapers, books, wallpaper, and floor boards as well. From the point of view of a hamster any of these items is fair game, but you will probably feel differently.

Important: Hamsters sometimes chew on electric cords. This is danger-ous not only for the animal but for the entire family.

If Your Hamster Escapes

Once a hamster senses release from the usual restraints on its move-ments—that is, once it realizes that it can run at will, it often develops the speed and agility of a weasel. Its alacrity becomes even greater once the room where it is allowed to run has become familiar. In strange surround-ings it may at first appear a little dazed, but once it has scouted out some hiding places, it can vanish from sight practically the moment you let go of it. Trying to entice it to come out again from behind a piece of furniture may be a challenge. My first hamster, whom I foolishly left unsupervised for just three minutes on a table in front of an open window, proceeded to make its way up the window frame onto the roof. There

In the photos:
The metal bars of the cage are often the scene of the wildest acrobatic activity. A hamster swings its way up and down effort-lessly, as if there were no such thing as gravity.

it ran along the gutter to the drain pipe. Whether it deliberately chose to chute down the pipe into the garden or slipped down unseen is not altogether clear. In any case, it had disappeared in the thick vegetation before it even crossed my mind that my hamster might no longer be in the room. A hamster's propensity to disappear is also the reason why you should never let your pet run free in your garden. It would instantly make for the bushes or burrow into the loose earth.

What to do: Please don't start on a wild, noisy chase when you realize your hamster is gone. You would only scare the animal and make retrieval more difficult. Even assuming that you succeeded, the animal would then be so upset that it would take endless time and patience to make it trust you again. It's much better to try to lure the escape artist back with a treat. If you don't know where the hamster might have headed, look in all the places that offer opportunities for climbing and hiding.

The "sunflower seed" trick: This method often works when you don't know where your hamster might have gone: Spread some sunflower seeds in every room, counting the number of seeds you leave in each room, and shut the doors. The next morning you will be able to tell easily which room the animal is in. Wherever the hamster is, the sunflower seeds will have disappeared. Now place the open cage in that room with a little trail of treats leading up to it.

Cleanliness in the Hamster Home

Hamsters are clean animals, and being clean is important to them. They set up a special place where they urinate and defecate, and they groom themselves frequently and thoroughly. They also don't have any offensive body odor the way white mice, for instance, do. Of course, feces and urine, as well as old food, begin to smell after a while. The better and the more often you clean out the cage, the less it will smell. The best place for the hamster while you clean the cage, as described below, is an empty pail or jar.

Daily: Clean out the bathroom corner (with an old spoon or a tiny trowel).

Weekly: Wash all accessories, such as food dish, seesaw, toys, and branches, with warm water. Scrub the water bottle with a bottle brush.

Twice a week: Change all the bedding (put the old bedding on the compost pile, or, if you don't compost, in the garbage). If your hamster's sleeping house doesn't have a floor, slide a thin board under it before picking it up. This way the food stores the hamster has stashed away there will not be disturbed (The Art of Laying in Supplies, page 31).

Once a month: Replace the sleeping nest (leave a bit of the old nesting material and supply new stuff). Wash the grating of the cage and the bottom pan with warm water.

Important: Don't use any detergents when cleaning the cage. Warm water is perfectly adequate.

Hamsters and Other Pets

Hamsters have no desire for contact with other pets and usually cannot be

This wooden structure is actually a toy designed for children, but it is easily turned into a jungle gym for a hamster. Just make sure it is well balanced and stands solidly so that it won't tip over when the hamster swings and jumps around on it.

If a hamster encounters an enemy that is obviously stronger, it drops onto its back and plays dead.

Dangers for a Hamster

Source of danger	Possible effects	How to avoid
Electric wires	Chewing and electrocution	Run wires behind wall; don't leave exposed wires under current; unplug when hamster runs free.
Stained or varnished wood	Can make hamster sick and is toxic if gnawed on	Prevent gnawing, distract hamster from it.
Vessels filled with water	Sliding in, drowning	Supervise hamster outside the cage.
Hot things	Burns	Don't let hamster run near stove or toaster.
Cage grating	Can escape if bars are too far apart; poisoning if metal is rusty	Watch for proper spacing of bars ($\frac{2}{5}$–$\frac{1}{2}$ in. or 1–1.3 cm). Replace rusted cage.
Ventilation shaft	Can escape	Supervise hamster outside the cage.
Human feet	Stepping on hamster	Supervise hamster outside the cage.
Plants	Poisoning, often fatal, if plants are toxic (ask florist or check in literature)	Don't keep poisonous plants where hamster might get at them.
Closets, drawers	Suffocating or starving if hamster is accidentally shut in	Put hamster back in its cage after its free run.
Chairs	Being squashed if someone sits down	Supervise hamster outside the cage.
Sun	Heat stroke	Never leave cage exposed to direct sun.
Pointed objects (needles, small nails)	Tearing cheek pouch if "stowed away"	Don't leave these things lying around.
Table	Falling; broken bones, internal injuries	Be careful not to let hamster escape from its cage.
Doors	Being caught and squashed in closing door	Keep doors closed while hamster is running free.

A short break during grooming. In a moment the hamster will lick its paws and wipe its face with them.

trained to live in the same space with them. I can only advise you not to try to combine them with other animals. There are exceptions, of course. But it is highly unlikely that your cat is the one in a thousand that resists regarding a hamster as its legitimate prey.

A cat or a dog may eat the hamster or is certainly likely to hurt it.

Large birds, like parrots, can pinch a hamster painfully.

Small birds, like parakeets and canaries, on the other hand, may get bitten by the hamster.

Introducing *other rodents*, such as mice, gerbils, and chipmunks, can lead to serious fights. If you do keep other species of rodents in addition to hamsters, please wash your hands with soap every time you change from handling one kind of animal to handling another. The scent of another rodent gets some hamsters so excited that they nip.

My tip: Let your hamster run free in the room only when the dog or cat is locked out. And make sure the hamster's cage is always securely locked.

What to Do during Vacations

An absence of one day: You can leave your hamster alone for a day or two without worry. Just give it plenty of dry food (for example, honeysticks, or grains and pellets), fill the water bottle with fresh water, and supply an apple or a fresh carrot for juicy snacks. And remember: A hamster's cage should never be left in glaring light, in the direct sun, or next to a radiator.

Longer absences: If you are going away for several days or weeks and can't or don't want to take your hamster along, you should make arrangements in good time. Neighbors, friends, relatives, or even your pet dealer can take over the simple chores. The hamster should always stay in its accustomed cage; this reduces the

stress of adjusting to a new human. It is useful to leave instructions behind that cover all the main points: what kind of food the hamster is used to, when the cage should be cleaned, whether the animal should be allowed to run free now and then. If the hamster is to be let out of its cage, this of course places a greater burden of responsibility on the caretaker.

When not to entrust your hamster's care to someone else: Pregnant or nursing hamster females react badly to changes in routine and

A hamster feels cozy and safe in the warm space created by two cupped hands whose smell is familiar.

should always be looked after by the person they know and trust. Otherwise the stress of adjustment might result in the mother hamster's eating her babies or refusing to nurse them.

Shying away from you: After a prolonged separation, your hamster may not recognize you again. With a little patience and a friendly, sensitive approach you will soon succeed in getting your pet to become tame and friendly again.

Hamsters don't have any body smell that is offensive to the human nose. But urine, feces, and old food do begin to smell after a while if the cage is not cleaned properly.

Taking the hamster along: If you are not traveling to the hot south and if your vacation accommodations allow it, you can take your hamster along. But be careful to protect it during the trip against drafts and direct sun. Set up the cage so that it doesn't wobble and the animal isn't shaken too much by the vehicle's motion. If you travel to foreign countries, ask your veterinarian or the consulate in question what, if any, documents you need. Have any necessary information translated into the language spoken where you are going to be, or you may run into trouble at the border.

Hamster Language

What you observe in your hamster	What the hamster is trying to tell you
Weight loss, apathy, dull fur, red eyes	I am sick or old.
Lying on the back, baring teeth	I'm scared. If you touch me, I'll resort to force.
Running away when being petted	I've had enough of this.
Busily collecting nesting material	I'm going to have babies and would like to be left alone.
Yawning	I feel pleasantly sleepy and comfortable.
Relaxed grooming, burrowing in the bedding, collecting food, lively acrobatics in the cage	I'm happy and content.
Irritability	I can't sleep in peace, and I get carried around too much.
Growling, muttering, squealing	I want to be left in peace.
Sitting up on the haunches	I've discovered something interesting
Passive, apathetic behavior	I'm bored. I need some stimulation.
Flinching	There was a noise that frightened me.

Proper Nutrition

The Art of Laying in Supplies

Hamsters are famous for hoarding food. In fact, the German word for hoarding is "hamstern."

Any hamster that is not on the point of starvation stuffs any food you give it into its cheek pouches and carries it either into its sleeping nest or to a clean corner of the cage—that is, to its food pantry. There everything is neatly sorted and stacked. This pantry is the hamster's sanctuary and should, theoretically, never be disturbed. But since a hamster, though endowed with a fine sense of cleanliness, can't tell which foods are perishable, you have

Any food is first of all stashed away in the cheeks.

to check the nest daily for moldy or rotting bits of food. To do this, use tweezers so that the food stores are disturbed as little as possible. After all, the storage supervisor will have to put everything back in order again after your intrusion.

My tip: If your hamster has given up sleeping in its house or is making a bed in a new place, check to see if the hoard inside the house is getting so large that there is not enough room left for sleeping.

What You Can Feed a Hamster

Getting food for a hamster is simple and inexpensive. Hamsters are not at all fussy and eat only little. Much of the food can be gathered from your garden or on nature walks. Always save a little bit for your pet when you get fruit and vegetables for your own meals. But please don't give your hamster garbage and leftover food. The better the quality of what you feed it, the better it is for your pet's health.

To provide your hamster with a varied, healthy diet you can choose from among many different things, ranging from dry pellets, and a mixture of various grains and seeds, to greens, succulent foods, honey, vegetable and egg sticks, puffs (with and without cheese), live food, and protein foods. Pet stores sell a great variety of suitable items. The more varied the things you offer, the merrier for the hamster—even if it doesn't touch some of the delectables.

Suitable Foods

Dry food: Commercial grain and seed mixtures and hamster pellets (available at pet stores); nuts, such as peanuts, filberts, and walnuts (all unsalted); cereal grains, such as wheat, oats, and corn; seeds (sunflower, pumpkin, hemp); rolled oats, and groats; honey, egg, and vegetable sticks; puffs, etc

Greens and succulent foods: Dandelion greens, chickweed, alfalfa, clover, meadow grass, sow thistle,

Recommended for hamsters: an upside-down water bottle with a tube, and a ceramic food dish.

31

Whether it be a section of an orange . . .

. . . or a grain bar, hamsters always enjoy a special treat.

common groundsel, shepherd's purse, cow parsnip; fruit of all kinds; vegetables, such as carrots (with the tops), cauliflower, potatoes (none of the leaves or sprouting eyes), tomatoes, spinach, celery, cucumbers, lettuce, and chicory.

Live food: Mealworms (available at pet stores).

Protein foods: Meat; cottage cheese (low-fat), yogurt (including fruit yogurt).

Other things: Drinking water; vitamin drops; fine hay. Twigs or branches from beech trees, maples, willows, hazelnut bushes, or fruit trees (for gnawing); dog biscuits.

Unsuitable (Poisonous) Foods

Raw beans; sprouting potato buds and green parts of potatoes as well as of tomatoes; fool's parsley; poison hemlock; laburnum; canned or frozen vegetables.

Ten Important Feeding Rules

1. Feed a varied diet.

2. Have food and water available not just in the evening but also during the day, that is, during the animal's somnolent period. Hamsters love to snack.

3. Give only fresh food of high quality.

4. Add vitamin drops for small mammals (sold by pet stores) to the food regularly. Amounts are suggested on package. Put the drops on mealworms or in yogurt.

5. Don't pick greens along roads with car traffic (exhaust fumes!), from meadows frequented by dogs (dog feces and urine contain bacteria), or along fields in agricultural use (possibly sprayed with chemicals).

6. Rinse vegetables, lettuce, and fruit from the supermarket and let the water drip off before giving the produce to the hamster.

7. Don't give a hamster cooked or fried food (table scraps!).

8. Avoid sudden changes in diet.

9. Keep the portions small (cut vegetables and fruit small); otherwise too much spoils.

10. All food should be at room temperature when given.

Dry Food

Dry food is the most important item on your hamster's menu. It should always be available as a basic staple. If you use commercial dry food sold by pet stores you can be sure that your

32

Variety is the secret for success. By offering many different kinds of food you ensure that your hamster will get all the nutrients it needs.

This juicy strawberry seems to be especially tasty.

33

Basic Menu Plan

(Dwarf hamsters need only half the amounts indicated.)

How often	What kind of food	What amounts
Daily	Grain mixture	$1/2$ oz. (15 g)
	Greens	1 small handful
	Succulent foods	As desired (e.g.,1 slice apple, 1 floret cauliflower)
	Mealworms	2–3
	Drinking water	Unlimited
Every 2 to 3 days	Meat	1 tiny piece
	Yogurt	1 teaspoon
	Cottage cheese	1 teaspoon
	Meadow hay	1 small handful
Once a week	Twigs for gnawing	As needed
	Dog biscuit	1 piece

F eeding a hamster is simple and inexpensive. Hamsters are not fussy about their food and require only small amounts of it. Much of it can come from your garden or be picked on walks in the countryside.

hamster is getting all the important nutrients it needs. These pellets, as well as commercial grain mixtures, contain protein, fat, carbohydrates, minerals, and vitamins in the proper proportions. It is very important to remember that a hamster that eats dry food exclusively always has to have drinking water available. Also, the food has to be stored in a dry place to keep from spoiling. If you compose your own mixture of dry foods (see page 31), make sure to use only ingredients in their natural state. That means, for instance, unroasted peanuts rather than the roasted and salted kind you buy for yourself; and don't give the hamster any of your own, sweetened breakfast cereal. Since you probably wouldn't enjoy a diet composed of nothing but dry foods, it is only reasonable that you not impose such a diet on your hamster either but instead give it something fresh and juicy every day.

Greens and Succulent Foods

With the help of wild greens, fruits, and vegetables it is easy to provide

With their clever paws hamsters can hold their food. They bite off piece after piece and stow it away in the cheek pouches.

variety in the daily menu. Greens and succulent foods are excellent sources of vitamins. Particularly during the summer, finding greens is no problem: You can get them out of your own garden or pick them on walks. Just make sure they are not contaminated with harmful substances (see page 32). If you don't want to take any chances, you can grow some grass indoors for your hamster. Pet stores sell small flats filled with soil already seeded. Fruit and vegetables, especially if bought at the supermarket, should be well rinsed with clear water and then dried because too much moisture can lead to diarrhea (see page 39).

It should go without saying that fruit that has been sprayed, such as oranges, is peeled before it is given to the hamster.

Live Food

In the wild, hamsters feed primarily on greens and various kinds of seeds, but they also eat small creatures, such as insects and their larvae, and occasionally even small birds. They are not purely vegetarian, as is often assumed, but omnivorous. This is something to take into account when you compose your hamster's meals. Apart from mealworms, crickets and grasshoppers are suitable for feeding to hamsters. But these latter two food animals are more difficult to keep.

Mealworms are the larvae of the darkling beetle, and any good pet store carries them. The best way to keep them is in a large canning jar half filled with raw oatmeal and covered with a small cloth. Keep the jar at room temperature (not next to a radiator or exposed to the sun). Place some fresh lettuce leaves and other vegetable leaves, washed and well dried, in the jar every other day. This supplies the larvae with the necessary vitamins. Don't worry if some of the larvae enter the pupal stage and even turn into

beetles—most hamsters will eat them quite readily all the same.

Important: Empty the jar from time to time, wash and dry it, fill it with fresh oatmeal, and put the live mealworms you have picked out back in the jar. If you don't do this, a mold will form that will make your hamster sick.

With stroking motions of the paws a hamster empties its cheeks of the food it has collected.

Protein Food

Meat: Your hamster will appreciate a tiny piece of raw lean meat (beef or veal) once or twice a week. Lean hamburger meat is best because the hamster can't choke on it.

Milk products: Hamsters also like cottage cheese and yogurt (including yogurt with fruit). Give a teaspoonful of cottage cheese or yogurt to your hamster regularly.

Important:
• Give only tiny portions of protein food that will be eaten up at once. Otherwise the cage gets too dirty.
• Never give these foods directly from the refrigerator.

To Keep the Teeth Healthy

Nuts, grains, and twigs provide a natural way of wearing down the incisor teeth. Dog biscuits also work well. Put a little piece in your hamster's cage. The biscuit will gradually be nibbled up and should then be replaced with a new piece. Pet stores also sell so-called

Special treats, such as carrots, grain, cauliflower, and walnuts are highly popular, and you should have some of them ready for your hamster.

Acrobatics on a hamster ladder:

With great agility the little fellow works its way upward...

small animal blocks. These supply the hamster with calcium and trace elements as well. Feed nuts only sparingly; they are very high in fat.

Meadow Hay for Eating and as Padding

In addition to the foods already mentioned, your hamster should always have some clean, dry hay. You can buy the hay or make it yourself (dry the mowed grass in the sun and store it in an airy place). As a food, hay is important for the hamster's digestion and overall health because it supplies roughage. But hamsters also like it for lining their nests.

Important: Hay has to be stored in a dry and airy place to keep it from getting moldy. Hay that has become moldy is poisonous.

The Right Amount of Food

A hamster needs about $1/2$ ounce (15 g) or 2 teaspoonfuls of mixed grains a day, plus 2 to 3 mealworms and plenty of fruit and vegetables or wild greens. Dwarf hamsters should get about half this amount. Whatever fresh food is not finished within 24 hours has to be taken out of the cage. Anything that could rot, get moldy, or spoil has to be removed. Dry grains, however, can be left without worry.

Drinking Water

Opinions and experiences relating to the need for drinking water vary widely. Many hamsters refuse to drink from a water bottle and get all the fluid they need from greens and succulent foods. Others get irritable if they don't have drinking water available at all times.

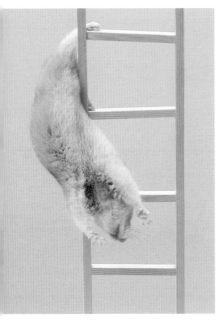

then hangs from a rung by its toes.

Time out to catch one's breath.

You can't go wrong if you offer your hamster water in an automatic water dispenser, and you will soon see what your hamster's preferences are. One thing that is beyond debate is that hamsters get thirstier on hot summer days and if they live in heated rooms. The best kind of water to give your hamster is uncarbonated mineral water.

Harmful for your hamster is water that is too strongly chlorinated or mineral water that is carbonated.

Hamsters as "Kitchen Helpers"

An acquaintance of mine has made it a habit to include her hamster in some of the kitchen chores. Thus "Julia" keeps her company when she cleans vegetables, waiting for a tidbit now and then. This could be some carrot greens, an overripe tomato, or anything else that humans usually don't eat. When Julia's cheek pouches are full, she is put back in her cage, where she quickly disappears into her pantry. This little game keeps both parties amused, but you have to be careful not to use your hamster as a dispose-all. Rotting parts of fruit or vegetables are taboo for the hamster, as are raw beans, sprouting potato eyes, green parts of potatoes and tomatoes, and foods meant exclusively for human consumption, such as chocolate.

In the photos:
A ladder is regarded as a challenge by hamsters. They will play around on it tirelessly, trying out the most varied climbing techniques.

What to Do if Your Hamster Gets Sick

Prevention Is Better Than Any Cure

If a hamster is kept under proper conditions and is given high-quality and varied food, it will often live beyond the normal life expectancy for its species, which is usually set at two years. My golden hamster dowager "Eugenia," for instance, enjoyed good health throughout her seven years (!) of life. Pathogens had a hard time trying to establish themselves in her healthy and resistant body.

Fruit is loaded with vitamins. But it has to be fresh, and it can't be left to rot in storage. That's why you have to check the sleeping house frequently and remove food that is going bad.

Hygiene is important: Bacteria, viruses, and worms can be transmitted to hamsters by other domestic animals, and even some human illnesses can in certain situations prove a danger to a hamster's health. That is why washing your hands before and after handling the animal is important.

Mistakes in care that can lead to sickness

- poor-quality food
- one-sided diet
- drafts
- abrupt temperature changes
- too much or too little air humidity
- damp bedding
- lack of opportunities for gnawing, climbing, and burrowing
- several hamsters that don't get along being kept together (stress!)
- disruptions during the sleeping period

First Signs of Illness

If you spend time every day with your hamster you are bound to notice any changes, such as if it suddenly stops climbing or eating or seems to be tired constantly (for other signs of illness, turn to the table on page 42). In an animal as small as a hamster, it is, unfortunately, often difficult to assess the seriousness of health problems, and illness progresses very rapidly. The few physical reserves the little body has are quickly exhausted. This is why you should take your hamster to the veterinarian as soon as you notice the first signs of illness. If you can't take the hamster right away, leave it in peace. Trying to actively "nurse" it would only upset the animal needlessly.

What to Do in Case of Colds

You can tell from its behavior if your hamster has caught a cold (from drafts, temperatures that are too high or too low, air that is too dry or too humid). The animal has a runny nose, its eyes tear, and interest in food declines. If you notice these symptoms, move the cage to a warm, draft-free spot (70° to 73° F or 21-23° C). If the hamster still doesn't eat, you should consult the veterinarian.

A hamster takes complete responsibility for its own cleanliness, but it is up to you to keep the cage in good sanitary order.

What to Do in Case of Diarrhea

Soft to runny feces are often a reaction to improper conditions or care, such as bad food, housing in quarters that are damp or too cool, dirty drinking water, or a diet based too exclusively on corn. To treat diarrhea, you should withdraw greens, fruit, and other foods high in moisture. Feed only grains, high-quality hay, and lukewarm camomile tea or very weak black tea (unsweetened!). If there is no improvement after one day, take the animal to the veterinarian. Don't confuse diarrhea with wet-tail, however! The animal's tail and anal area, and often parts of the belly, are damp or soiled with soft excrements. See your veterinarian immediately. He will prescribe an antibiotic to be given in the drinking water.

Conditions Due to Faulty Heredity

All pet hamsters alive today are descended from only three animals (see History of a Meteoric Rise, page 51). But hamsters have coped surprisingly well with the hereditary abnormalities that such a limited gene pool is likely to give rise to. Nevertheless, strains and single animals do turn up now and then where "something has gone wrong." Perhaps a hamster loses its hair prematurely, or it develops tumorlike growths, or some of its

To make sure that vitamin supplements end up in the hamster's stomach and not in its hidden food stash, the drops should be added to food that is eaten right away. Mealworms are especially good for this purpose.

Health Check

	In a healthy hamster	In a sick hamster
Eyes	Bright and shiny, no discharge	Inflamed, fur around eye sticky
Coat	Thick, with a silky sheen	Disheveled, dull
Anal region	Clean	Smeared with fecal matter
Body shape	Evenly cylindrical	Sides caved in
Nose	Dry	Damp
Behavior	Lively, alert	Disinterested, apathetic

Hamsters manage to conquer chunks of food . . .

. . . that are almost as big as they are.

meningitis, or LCM) is a mouse disease that is transmitted to young golden hamsters in poorly controlled breeding stations. It has never been observed in dwarf hamsters. The affected animals lose weight, become sleepy, move slowly, and their fur becomes shaggy. Conjunctivitis, which often accompanies the disease, makes light painful to the sick animal's eyes. However, after three weeks the animals usually recover.

This form of meningitis can spread to humans, but it is usually no more harmful to them than a slight incidence of flu. Serious cases are rare. Still, as a precaution, you should visit your doctor if you have flu-like symptoms.

If you want to be entirely safe, ask your pet-store manager to provide you with a young hamster from a known LCM-free stock (unfortunately, these animals are still very rare).

Important: Pregnant women are strongly urged not to keep young hamsters because the disease can lead to premature birth and to malformations in the fetus. If you have had a hamster for some time and it is at least five months old, however, there is no danger. Of course, LCM-free animals must be housed in a mouse-free environment to avoid new infections!

Visits to the Veterinarian

The best time to take your hamster is afternoon or evening. If possible, transport the hamster in its cage, with a cloth draped over it to keep drafts out. If the cage is too large, use an appropriate box and put some of the hamster's bedding and nest into it. Please don't take only fresh bedding with you. In most cases the veterinarian will need a stool sample for the purpose of diagnosing the problem.

Giving Medications

Some medications are administered by the veterinarian in the form of injections, but some you may have to

movements are abnormal. Hamsters that suffer from severe conditions should be put to sleep by the veterinarian; no hamster with any abnormality should ever bred.

Danger of Contagion for Humans

Diseases of hamsters caused by improper living conditions are of no danger to humans. The same is not always true of infectious diseases that may have been transmitted to the hamster by other animals. Meningitis, for instance, (lymphocytic chorio-

give yourself. This is not an easy task. Even if your hamster normally eats whatever you place in front of it, it is not likely to cooperate when you approach with medications. You will need to be resourceful. Dissolve the powder or dilute liquids in the drinking water, or add the medication to a favorite treat the hamster takes from your hand (mealworm, cottage cheese, meat). This way you have some assurance that the medication is actually swallowed because these treats are eaten up on the spot rather than stuffed into the cheeks to be deposited inside the house, where other medicated food is likely to remain, untouched.

Disinfecting

Sometimes, as in the case of diarrhea, it is necessary to disinfect the hamster's living quarters. Wash the cage and all the accessories thoroughly with warm water. Then disinfect everything, following the directions that come with the product that has been recommended to you by the druggist or the pet dealer. Finally, rinse cage and accessories with warm water, let them dry well, and set the cage up again the way you do after an ordinary cleaning.

Death from Old Age

I have watched many a hamster grow old, but I am still saddened each time I see one weak with age and near death. Old hamsters sleep a lot and leave their nest only for eating and an occasional little outing. They lose weight and walk on tottering legs. Sometimes they also become blind, which is not tragic, however, because their sense of smell is sufficient for them to navigate by. These old animals are usually not in pain. Just give your old hamster the kind of food it likes, if it is still eating, and leave it alone otherwise. Within a few days it will go to sleep and not wake up again.

No effort is considered too great to get at tasty food.

Diseases

What you notice	Possible causes you can remedy yourself	Likely diagnosis and treatment by veterinarian
Apathetic behavior	Environment too cold (hiberation)	Could be anything, possibly an infection.
Bald spots	One-sided diet	Deficiency symptom
Weight loss	Too little food	Sign of old age or symptom of some disease.
Soft to runny stool (with sour smell)	Bad food, damp bedding, drafts, being too cool, one-sided diet, intestinal infection	Diarrhea; wet-tail
Sneezing, rasping breathing	Temperature too cold or hot, air too dry or humid, drafts	Pneumonia
Refusal of food	Conditions that are too cool and damp, overheating, drafts. Abnormal position of teeth (after a fall or overgrowth), injury to cheek pouch	A cold; overgrown teeth; wound in cheek pouch
Overgrown teeth, overgrown claws	Lack of opportunity to dig and climb	Teeth or claws have to be corrected by veterinarian.
Light bleeding, wounds with scabs	Injury from pointed objects or from fights between rivals	Dab minor injuries with tincture of iodine (wear gloves for safety's sake); take animal with serious wounds to veterinarian.
Limping; dragging one leg	A fall or having been shoved	Contusion or fracture
Avoidance of light	Conjunctivitis caused by draft or dusty bedding	Inflammation of the eyes, possibly meningitis (LCM, see p. 40).
Continual scratching, inflamed skin	Unsanitary conditions, poor care, parasites picked up from other pets	Parasites, fungi

If Your Hamster Has Babies

About Unplanned Breeding

I got my first hamster babies the proverbial way a virgin gets pregnant. A friend brought along his golden hamster on a visit. He assured me it was a female, just like my "Eugenia." We put the two hamsters in a cage together and went outside to play cowboys and Indians. In the evening my friend went home with "Minni." When it occurred to me to wonder, two weeks later, why Eugenia never seemed to emerge from her nest anymore and I looked to check on her, I found I now had seven golden hamsters. My first task was to enlighten my friend about the facts of life.

I'm sure I'm not the only one who has had this kind of experience. Tales of such "accidents" are commonplace whenever hamster owners swap stories. The next step is just as typical: The mislabeled hamster is renamed ("Minni" became "Prince Eugene"), and the baby hamsters are palmed off with much rhetorical finesse on school mates. Anyone who has ever been inadvertently blessed with baby hamsters is a little more cautious the next time someone wants to come visiting with a hamster.

Breeding for Specific Colors

I have already described some of the color varieties of golden hamsters, however there are many more. In England and in the United States, hamster fanciers have organized clubs and display their animals in shows. There you can find gray, blue, yellow, and black hamsters, to mention just a few. The quick succession of genera-tions in hamsters makes it possible to breed new colors in a relatively short time.

Perhaps you have a desire to learn more about how the laws of genetics

In these two dangling acrobats the distinguishing sexual charac-teristics are easy to see. The male (left) has a more pointed tail end, and the space between the anus and the genital opening is clearly larger than in the female (right).

work in the case of hamsters and to try to create a new color. Be fully aware, though, that this is a demanding hobby. Apart from suitable rooms and a large number of cages, you need some capital to start out with, patience, sensitivity toward animals, trustworthy takers for the hamsters' offspring, and, above all, time. Weekend trips and, especially, longer vacations become problematical because it won't be easy to find knowledgeable and conscien-

This hamster mother is diligently licking her baby clean.

After any short outing it is important to

tious caretakers. A period of negligent care can result in an epidemic of disease and mass dying.

If you want to become a conscientious breeder, the first thing you have to do is to read some books to familiarize yourself thoroughly with the laws of genetics. If you are lax in this respect, you may end up producing nonviable, malformed animals.

The Desire for Baby Hamsters

Since raising hamsters on a large scale is out of the question for the average hamster owner, I am going to base my remarks on the assumption that you would simply like to watch your hamsters have babies once. For this purpose you may want to start out with a pair of hamsters. Remember, however, that once two hamsters have taken a liking to each other, there will be a great number of offspring in a very

short time. Theoretically, a single pair can give rise to a population of several thousand within a single year. This amazing fertility is due to the short gestation period (the shortest of all mammals), the great readiness to mate, and the early sexual maturity of hamsters (see Breeding Data, page 50).

What to Do with the Young

This is a question that has to be solved before you let your two hamsters so much as sniff each other. Explore the possibilities in good time, for a hamster family can stay together only for a limited time. Either the animals will start fighting or the cage will get too crowded. And be prepared for additional litters if the family members are not separated early enough. As you can see, finding homes in good time is crucial. Relatives and

sniff each other again.

A baby found outside the nest is promptly carried back.

friends are possible takers, and a pet dealer might be able to help you out.

Selection of Parent Animals

The breed: If you are getting a pair for the purpose of mating them and are still relatively inexperienced with hamsters, I would recommend dwarf hamsters or Russian or cream-colored golden hamsters. These hamsters are usually so pacific that the male and the female can be kept together even while the babies are born and suckled. Your best bet is to get two healthy, recently weaned young hamsters from the same litter. If at all feasible, they should never be separated. Of course you have to have a cage that is large enough for two animals (at least 20 × 14 × 12 inches or 50 × 35 × 30 cm). It is also useful to have two separate sleeping houses with tops that either flip up or can be lifted off. Wild-type

and piebald golden hamsters are usually better kept in separate quarters.

The best age: In littermates that have grown up together sexual maturity usually sets in relatively late. If you are going to mate unrelated hamsters, make sure they are old enough. The female should be at least two months old (for dwarf hamsters, four months). Females that have babies too young often don't have enough milk for them. In many cases they also tend to eat the young (see Cannibalism, page 47). The male should be at least a month older than the female.

Ready to Mate or Not?

In the relatively rare cases where a pair of hamsters can be kept together all the time, babies will at some point appear quite automatically. You have nothing to do with it. However, things are different if you place two hamsters

In the photos:
For the first ten days baby hamsters are completely dependent on their mother. She nurses and cleans them and makes sure that they are warm enough.

45

that don't know each other in the same cage. Female hamsters that are sexually receptive are willing to mate only every fifth or sixth day. On the other days the female bites the male, or buck, to drive him away. It is your job, therefore, to stand by, armed with gloves, when you introduce the pair. If there is trouble, you have to intervene

To check the nest you cautiously move aside some of the nesting material. Use a twig from inside the cage for this because it smells familiar.

immediately and separate the animals before the buck sustains too many bites. Don't be disappointed if your first effort fails, and try again the next evening. From 8 to 11 P.M. is the most promising time.

My tip: Place the female in the male's cage, not the other way around. In her accustomed environment the female would be even more aggressive and might seriously injure the buck.

Courtship and Mating

The two partners communicate with each other by means of scent signals (see page 57). When the female is

placed in the buck's cage, she immediately starts marking it with a secretion from her genitals, which she presses hard against the floor. The secretion smells different, depending on whether the female is in heat or not. The buck instantly understands the signal. If he gets the green light, he starts his courtship immediately, licking his lady's head and ears, nudging her with his muzzle, and stroking her buttocks. First one animal and then the other rolls over on its back to let the other sniff its abdomen and genitals. Periodically the female gets up and runs away from the buck, as though to prolong the courtship phase. However, she never goes far, and the buck usually has no trouble keeping up with her, holding his nose close to the glands on her side. Eventually he tries to lift up the female's rear end by pushing with his muzzle until she stops and stands rigidly still, her back concave. Now he can mount her. Immediately after copulation, the rigidity leaves her, and she urges the male to renewed activity by batting him. The whole thing is repeated several times, until the female has had enough. As soon as she starts fighting the buck off, you have to separate the two animals.

Gestation, a Period of Special Care

You will soon be able to tell whether or not the mating was successful. You will know not so much because of the increase in the female's girth, which is very minor and therefore hard to detect for a novice hamster keeper, but because of her changed behavior. She starts hoarding more than ever and digging around in her nest, busily carrying nesting material in and out. She is obviously reconditioning it and lining the inside with fresh, soft padding. If she deems the sleeping house too small to serve as nursery, she will build a separate birthing nest outside.

Some females are more nervous and jumpy at this time than usual.

What you should do during the gestation period

• Make plenty of nesting material available.
• Be especially calm and gentle when handling the expectant mother.
• Don't let strangers near her.
• Avoid loud noises.
• Feed a diet rich in vitamins and proteins.
• Change the bedding one last time two days before the due date (don't touch the nest!). Then leave the female completely alone except for feeding her.

The Longed-for Day Arrives

Most likely you are looking forward to the happy event with eager anticipation and would love to witness the birth of the hamster babies. But please don't act on your desires. The female must not be disturbed while she is giving birth, nor for several hours afterwards. In most cases, the first sign you have of the birth having taken place is that the female fails to emerge from her nest at the accustomed time. If your hearing is very acute, you might be able to detect the high-pitched squeaks of the babies.

The birth process: The birth usually takes place at night and hardly ever takes more than a half hour. The female assumes a squatting position and waits for the first young to pop out. When it does, she picks it up with her front paws and rips the amniotic sac open with her incisor teeth, eating the membrane and the afterbirth. Then she bites off the umbilical cord and licks the baby clean. A few minutes later the process is repeated with the next baby.

Cannibalism

Not long ago I received a sad letter from a young hamster owner. She was upset and outraged because her

otherwise nice and well-behaved female hamster had eaten three of her babies shortly after they were born. I explained to my young correspondent that in small mammals eating their young is not all that rare an occurrence. In nature this happens primarily when too many individuals of the same species inhabit a given area. It is nature's way to prevent overcrowding and to make sure that there is enough space and food for those that live. In captive hamsters cannibalism may be caused by one of the following:

Too frequent breeding: There should always be a pause of at least about six weeks between litters, and no female should be expected to breed more than six times.

Hungrily the baby hamsters crowd to the teats. They knead the mother's mammary glands with their front paws, thus stimulating the milk flow.

Protein deficiency: This condition arises if the female has not been given enough protein-rich food during the gestation period or if she is too young. Females that are not yet fully developed physically need a great deal of protein.

Stillborn or weak young: When the mother bites through the umbilical cord she proceeds to eat the end hanging off

Baby hamsters are almost always born during the night. It takes only half an hour for all the young of a litter to be born, freed from the amniotic membrane, and have the umbilical cord chewed off.

47

Hamsters are combative when it comes to defending their territory. Fights inside a cage usually end in blood. But if the contestants have enough space, the loser can escape before it's too late.

Two hamsters rising up on their hind legs—a battle may be in the offing.

the baby. An instinctive mechanism makes her stop nibbling when she gets to the baby's navel. The baby normally squeals in protest when the umbilical cord is pulled, and these squeals stop the mother from chewing any farther. If the baby fails to squeal because it is weak or has been born dead, the mother simply keeps on eating.

Changes in the environment: Nervous or jumpy hamster females sometimes eat their young as late as a week after birth if they are upset. That is why you have to treat the hamster mother with extreme care and change nothing inside her cage. Until the young are at least one week old, only the person she is used to should approach the cage, and nothing more should be done than changing the litter in the corner used for urinating. Don't replace the nesting material until the young have left the cage, that is, after three to four weeks at the earliest.

Cautious Nest Check

You should briefly peek into the nest every evening to make sure that all is

48

well—dead babies have to be removed right away—but make sure you do it at a moment when the mother is not present. Otherwise she will be very agitated. If she has not already left the nest, lure her out with a favorite treat. Please, never reach into the nest with your fingers. The smell thus introduced would be highly upsetting to the mother hamster. Use a small twig from the cage that smells familiar to the animal (see drawing, page 46).

Care of the Young

Hamster babies are typical nidicolous creatures, that is, they are born naked, blind, and totally dependent on their mother, who nurses them, keeps them warm, and licks them clean.

Nursing: During the first few days after giving birth, the female hardly leaves her young at all. She lies there in typical nursing position with one hind leg raised to keep her body weight from crushing any of the babies, and the babies instinctively find their way to the seven to eleven pairs of nipples, arranged in a double row. Once the connection is made, they hang on tight, kneading their mother's belly as they nurse. This massaging motion stimulates the milk flow.

Keeping warm: When, after a few days, the mother starts leaving the nest, she covers the still hairless young with nesting material. If she didn't do this, the little hamsters might die of hypothermia.

Keeping clean: An important part of the mother's care of her young is licking them. Licking not only keeps them clean but also encourages the elimination of feces and urine. The mother then eats up the little droppings, thus keeping the nest clean.

Transporting the Young

Now and then tiny and still helpless hamster babies end up outside the nest. This can happen if, for instance, a

The front paws are used for self-defense.

The gray hamster seems to be winning dominance.

baby hangs on to the mother's teat when she leaves the nest for some reason and then lets go. When dropped, the baby hamster calls for help with feeble peeps that are almost inaudible to the human ear. The mother immediately picks up the little one with her front teeth by whatever part of the body presents itself and carries it back into the nest. The baby hamster meanwhile keeps absolutely still while being carried, assuming the rigidity typical of young mammals in this situation. Sometimes, too, really tiny

49

baby hamsters are transported by the mother in her cheek pouches. But this method is used only if danger is imminent and speed is of the essence. This habit of carrying the young back to the nest is instinctive and shared by many mammals. Right after the birth of the young the instinct is so strong that it is sometimes acted out with surrogate objects. Rats, for instance, have been observed during this phase grabbing hold of their own tail repeatedly and trying to carry and deposit it in the nest. Sometimes they even take hold of one of their hind legs and limp back to the nest on three legs.

If it is necessary to move the young, the mother picks them up with her teeth and the baby assumes a characteristic rigidity while being carried.

Development of the Young

Day of birth: Hairless, reddish skin, and undeveloped, weak limbs; eyes shut. Staggering, crawling movements on hind legs spread wide. Elimination of feces and urine only after abdominal massage by the mother.

From 2nd day on: First pigment formation; body skin turns dark.

From 5th day on: Mother brings food back to nest. Babies start nibbling on food. Thin coat of hair forms. First grooming motions while lying on the belly.

From 10th day on: Eyes are open.

Cheek pouches are filled and emptied. Sitting posture assumed for grooming, but frequent loss of balance. Independent urinating and defecating.

From 14th day on: First independent ventures outside the nest. Playing with siblings.

21st day: Complete independence.

The Time to Leave Approaches

At two to three weeks the baby hamsters begin to play, and at this stage they are an absolute delight to watch. Standing on wobbly legs, they pair off to engage in comical wrestling matches, or they may roll across the cage head over heels one after the other.

The temptation to keep all the baby hamsters is strong at this point. But that's not possible, and it is time to ask their future owners to get everything ready for the arrival of their new charges.

Breeding Data at a Glance

Sexual maturity: at 5 to 6 weeks

Sexual cycle: 5 to 6 days

Age for first breeding: *Golden hamsters*: 8 to 9 weeks for females; 12 to 13 weeks for males; *Dwarf hamsters*: 3 to 4 months

Gestation: *Golden hamsters*: 16 to 18 days; *Dwarf hamsters*: 19 to 22 days

Litter size: *Golden hamsters*: 6 to 10; *Dwarf hamsters*: 5 to 6

Number of teats: 7 to 11 pairs

Nursing period: 15 to 21 days

Separation of young from mother (and segregation by sex): on 21st day

Understanding Hamsters

Almost everything we know about hamsters derives from observation of captive animals. Research on hamsters in the wild is problematical. Even finding their burrows is difficult, and observing these small, nocturnal creatures in the dark is practically impossible. In this chapter I shall try to shed some light on the most important aspects of the behavior and the way of life of hamsters. Most of my remarks will be restricted to the Syrian or golden hamster.

History of a Meteoric Rise

The golden hamster's rise to popularity as a pet and laboratory animal is quite unique. Golden hamsters were first discovered in 1839 by the British zoologist George Waterhouse near the Syrian city of Aleppo. Waterhouse called the animal he had discovered *Cricetus auratus* or, translated into English, golden hamster. Then nothing more was heard about this pretty rodent for almost a hundred years. The only thing to prove the existence of the animal was one pelt, which could be admired in the British Museum. In 1930, Professor I. Aharoni of the Zoology Department of the University of Jerusalem once more focused attention on the hamster. In the course of an excursion to the Syrian desert with his students, he came across the burrow of a female golden hamster with eight young. He dug up the animals and took them along. Unfortunately only three of them survived the trip and the unaccustomed conditions of captivity. The surviving hamsters were taken to the Zoological

Institute of Jerusalem, where they multiplied so rapidly that by the end of the year their number had increased to 300. At this point the animals were given the scientific name by which they are known today, *Mesocricetus auratus*, or, literally translated, medium-sized golden hamster. The size is included in the Latin name because golden hamsters are smaller than common hamsters (*Cricetus*) but larger than dwarf hamsters (*Cricetulus*). The

A common hamster sniffing the air. It is making sure there is no danger around.

Hamsters living in the wild keep busy all summer gathering and stowing away food for winter. They sometimes amass astonishing quantities. In one case, 38 pounds (17 kg) of grain were found in the burrow of a common hamster. That is 60 times the animal's own weight.

vernacular name is Syrian or golden hamster.

Since the hamsters quickly adapted to life in a cage, were easy to take care of, and were highly fertile, they began to be used as laboratory animals in medical research. Later on, they became popular as pets, first in

51

This tempting treat is worth standing up for.

threatened, or if they fear for their food stores or their own safety. The common hamster suffers from a bad reputation for other reasons as well. It is considered a serious pest because it steals grain harvested by farmers and hoards it in burrows for consumption during the winter. This habit has resulted in efforts at elimination so successful that common hamsters are now very rare and have been declared a protected species. Most people know common hamsters only from pictures. In the wild, hamsters disappear into their burrows the instant they sense the approach of their presumed enemy. But I have heard one story of a person who was attacked by an irate hamster, which clung fiercely to his leg, because he had inadvertently come too close to the animal's burrow when out walking.

Where it is found: Grain fields in western, central, and southeastern Europe and in Asia offer protection and food to the common hamster. What hamsters need to thrive is soil that is dry, relatively firm, and fertile. In areas that are too sandy, the burrows would collapse, and where the soil is too heavy or has too many rocks, digging is too arduous.

What it looks like: The common hamster measures about 10 inches (25 cm) and has very short legs, a pointed head, and strong paws. It also has a dark belly, which is an unusual feature. In mammals the underparts of the body are normally lighter than the top, a color pattern that makes sense because it serves the purpose of camouflage. If the side of the body that is exposed to the light is darker than the shaded ground on which the animal moves, the contours are harder to see. The hamster, however, being active only in the twilight and at night, has no need for this disguising color pattern. Hamsters sit up on their haunches to scent the wind and to appear more intimidating (see page 58), and in this

America, and, since 1945, in Europe as well.

The Common Hamster

Another hamster species, the common or black-bellied hamster of Europe (*Cricetus cricetus*; see drawing on page 51) is unfortunately becoming quite rare. That is the hamster that appears in fables and children's stories. "Mean as a hamster" is a common expression in Germany, but one that does the animal an injustice. Hamsters become "mean" only if they feel

position the dark underparts make it harder to detect the animals in the surrounding darkness.

Special Anatomical Features

Strong teeth: Like almost all rodents, hamsters have 16 teeth: 2 incisors and 6 molars in each jaw. The chisel-shaped incisors don't have roots and therefore never stop growing. The act of eating keeps them constantly sharp. The chewing musculature is highly developed in hamsters, which makes them extremely efficient at gnawing.

The cheek pouches: These are capacious skin pockets that reach from the inside of the lips down to the shoulders and serve primarily for transporting food that is not consumed on the spot. The dimensions of these pockets are such that the size of the head is doubled when the pouches are filled to capacity. Up to $2/3$ ounce (18 g) of food can be stowed in them. The hamster then repairs to its storage chamber, where it strokes its paws along the cheeks to empty them. No digestive activity takes place inside the cheeks. The pouches are not used solely for transport of food and of the young (see page 49) but also have a useful function in defense against enemies. When trying to intimidate an opponent, a hamster often puffs up the pouches with air to make itself seem larger, which may move the antagonist to retreat.

Legs and toes: The front legs of a golden hamster are strong and muscular. They are equipped with four toes and a rudimentary thumb. These paws are used for digging, climbing, and doing acrobatics. The hind legs, which are equipped with five well-developed toes, are weaker. They shovel back the earth that is loosened in the course of burrowing and serve as support for climbing.

The stomach: Another feature that

First of all, lets sniff to find out what this is.

One is nibbling already while the other is still busy checking.

hamsters share with other rodents is a double-chambered stomach. The food is predigested in the larger first chamber and then completely broken down in the main stomach.

Sensory Capacities

Vision: Hamsters have relatively large eyes that are slightly protruding, as in most nocturnal animals. They are farsighted but don't see with great sharpness. However, the lateral position of the eyes gives hamsters a fairly wide angle of vision (about 110

53

degrees), enabling them to spot enemies in good time.

Hearing: The sense of hearing is well developed in hamsters. It seems likely that they hear sounds in the ultrasonic range. At least it has been shown that baby hamsters utter cries in that sound range, which wouldn't make sense if the mother were unable to hear the cries. Also, hamsters flinch when high-pitched or squealing noises, which almost always include sounds of ultrahigh frequencies, are produced in their vicinity. The hearing of hamsters is also highly differentiated. Thus any hamster learns very quickly to tell its caretaker's voice from other human voices.

Sense of touch: A hamster uses its whiskers (vibrissa) to explore its immediate surroundings. Its whiskers tell it if there are obstacles in its path and whether or not a certain passage is wide enough to fit through. Whiskers thus constitute an excellent tactile organ.

Hamsters have two chisel-shaped front teeth in the upper and in the lower jaws. These teeth keep growing throughout life but are kept at proper lengh through continual gnawing.

Description of a Golden or Syrian Hamster
(*Mesocricetus auratus*)

Order: Rodentia.

Suborder: Myomorpha.

Family: Cricetidae.

Subfamily: Cricetus.

Length of body: Male, 6³/₄ in. (17 cm); female, 7 in. (18 cm).

Length of tail: ¹/₂ in. (1.2 cm).

Weight: Male, 4.2–6 oz. (120–170 g); female, 5.3–6.3 oz. (150–180 g).

Way of life: Solitary, nocturnal steppe dweller.

Life expectancy: 2 to 4 years.

Geographic origin: Syria.

Domestication: Since 1930.

Sense of smell: The hamster's sense of smell is also highly developed. Hamsters live in a world of smells. Their whole concept of their surroundings, of enemies, and of sexual partners, is based on smell, not on appearance, as with us.

Friendly relations between a pair of animals can turn into instant and ferocious enmity if one of the partners is temporarily removed, placed in a different enviroment, carried around by humans, or combined with another hamster. It is important for hamster owners to be aware of this fact and to see to it that the group scent shared by animals that have been coexisting peacefully and that are to stay together is not obliterated.

The group scent is altered even when two hamsters living in the same cage are separated by a wire-mesh partition that keeps them from engaging in mutual grooming and sleeping nestled together. After a period of such segregation, females from the same litter are impossible to combine again, and a male and a female readjust to each other only after repeated and very patient tries to bring them together again.

A Passion for Grooming

Hamsters spend a big part of their waking time grooming themselves. Every hamster cleans itself meticulously from head to toe when it first wakes up and again later, more cursorily. To reach all parts of the body, it uses the tongue, the teeth, the paws, and the toenails and goes through the most comical contortions.

Why hamsters groom themselves: This preoccupation with external appearance has nothing to do with vanity. The primary purpose of grooming is to keep the fur in good condition, for only fur that is untangled and arranged properly will keep such a small body warm. The body loses less heat if the fur lies smooth with many tiny spaces between the hairs where air is trapped. When a hamster becomes very agitated, as during conflict situations, it will sometimes suddenly start washing its face furiously. Ethologists call this kind of behavior "displacement activity."

How hamsters groom themselves: Usually a hamster does not sit upright like a squirrel to groom itself but leans more heavily on its rear end. Generally the cleaning begins with the head. With circular motions the front paws pass along the tongue, which is stuck out. Then the paws rub repeatedly first across the muzzle and afterwards over the entire head, brushing against the lay of the hair. Every few seconds the paws are licked again. Next come the abdomen, the back, arms and legs. Getting at some of these places requires acrobatic stretching and twisting. Finally the hamster resorts to its teeth and hind paws to reach spots that are inaccessible to the front paws.

Why Hamsters Hoard

As a safety measure: Many small rodents that are subject to attack from many predators share the hamster's way of gathering food but not eating it until they can do so in safety. We don't know exactly what animals prey on golden hamsters in their native Syria, but no doubt there are many of them.

Where the front paws won't reach for grooming, the hind feet are resorted to.

Vocal Expression

Utterance	What it means
Hissing	Threatening sound made when attacking or during courtship
Screeching	Sound of defense and expression of great fear when threatened by an enemy or predator
Teeth chattering	Aggression; an urgent warning addressed to an enemy
Squealing	Aggression; accompanies minor fighting
Growling, muttering	Aggression; uttered by the male after copulation
Squeaking	Sound made by baby hamsters when they feel abandoned

Otherwise these tremendously fertile creatures would be so numerous in their homeland that one would trip over them constantly at night. Basically any carnivore larger than the Syrian hamster itself—including foxes, cats, martens, as well as owls and most hawklike birds—is a potential enemy of these rodents.

As provisions for winter: What is remarkable about hamsters is that they systematically stockpile food for consumption in bad times. Their burrows include separate storage chambers, which the animals fill with special diligence in autumn. Dwarf hamsters that live in the wild have to collect enough food during this season to last them seven to nine months. Hamsters are extremely particular in the selection of their winter food. Only ripe seeds are picked. These are carefully sorted, and any slightly rotten

Food envy in hamsters.

A wild pursuit is about to take place.

parts and bits of hull removed. Even live food is stored. Thus, a winter food stash belonging to a dwarf hamster has been found that contained 40 different beetles, 4 fly larvae, and 15 spiders. All these insects were in a state of hibernation—in the freezer, so to speak. The amounts collected by common hamsters are also quite staggering. One animal's burrow yielded 37 pounds (17 kg) of grain. That is about 60 times the animal's own weight. Quite an accomplishment!

A Loner by Nature

Hamsters are considered solitary animals. Ethologists call animals solitary if they avoid contact with others of their species except during the mating season, that is, if they react toward each other aggressively and don't live in pairs or groups.

Wild hamsters establish and aggressively defend their territories against intruders. A female accepts the presence of a male only for mating and then proceeds to raise her young by herself. She cares for them well and lovingly until, after three or four weeks, they can fend for themselves. Then she drives them away by biting them.

One reason for this solitary way of life may be the scarceness of food supplies in the hamster's natural environment. Steppes and deserts don't abound in plant and animal life. Thus, other members of the species become competitors for the available food. Domestication and selective breeding have produced some less belligerent breeds, and hamsters belonging to these more tolerant strains can be kept in pairs and coexist peacefully.

Ferocious Fighters

Hamsters guard their territory with fierce energy. In nature, hamster fights hardly ever get bloody because the loser can flee the battle scene before it is too late. In a small cage, however, the weaker party hardly ever survives a serious fight. To explore the territorial behavior of hamsters the following experiment was conducted:

Two male golden hamsters were kept under conditions resembling those of their natural environment in an enclosed area of about 800 square feet (7.5 sq m), where they could dig and burrow at will. The first week each animal was left alone in its half the area

Finally the booty has to be shared.

so that it could get used to the new place and mark it with its scent by spreading a secretion from glands on the sides of the body. As soon as the door in the partition between the two areas was opened, a bitter fight ensued. The weaker hamster eventually fled back to its own side of the partition, but it led a miserable life there from that point on. It hardly dared venture beyond the immediate surroundings of its burrow and was thus unable to gather many food supplies. It left very few scent marks and those were all very close to its nest.

The superior animal, on the other hand, moved freely wherever it wished, collected a huge hoard of food, and marked territory frequently, especially around the burrow of the vanquished animal. The latter would initially try to defend its nest but then usually ran away when its opponent penetrated anyway.

How Hamsters Communicate

Thanks to their extraordinary olfactory capacities, hamsters are able to express moods and leave "messages" for their fellows by means of scent secretion. They have special glands that produce a secretion that is used to mark territory. After extensive sniffing, a hamster will proceed to mark especially those places where another hamster has previously left its scent mark.

The glands producing the secretion are located on the sides of the body in golden hamsters. The same is true for many other burrowing animals. This way they are able to mark even the most narrow crevices they squeeze through. Chinese hamsters have glands not only on the side but also on the abdomen (ventral glands), and Dzjungarian dwarf hamsters have only ventral glands. Females in heat mark their territory with secretions from their genital organs, which they press hard against the ground in the process of marking. This is a sign to the males. Now they know that they can approach this particular female without danger of being attacked. A female not in heat also dots the ground with scent marks from the vagina if a male approaches. If the male persists in following her, she marks very frequently and thoroughly at short intervals until the male gives up. If he doesn't get the point, she gets ready to reinforce it with her nails.

In the photos:
Contests over food morsels are always playful in nature. They never degenerate into serious fighting.

57

Body Language

What the hamster does	What it means
Creeping along close to the ground	Insecurity in unfamiliar surroundings
Puffing up cheeks	Intimidation
Extensive, relaxed grooming	Sense of comfort and being at peace
Yawning	Sense of comfort, feeling relaxed
Raising both front paws	Readiness for defense in a female when attacked by a male
Leaping into the air	Good mood, high spirits
Sitting up on the haunches	Attention or aggression
Ears pointing backward	Feeling tired or insecure; fear, bad mood, aggressiveness, attention
Lying on the back motionless	Posture of defense; fear
Walking on stiff legs, tail pointing straight up	Fear, posture of subordination, appeases older or stronger members of the species
Stretching	Sense of comfort, feeling relaxed
Sudden, prolonged grooming	Being startled
Folded ears	Attention
Sudden flinching	Being startled or frightened

How Hamsters Cope with Enemies

Sniffing the air: When a hamster detects some suspicious sound, it rises up on its haunches and sniffs the air. The greater the sensed danger, the higher up the animal rises and the longer it sniffs—sometimes several seconds at a time. If there are no further signs of danger, the hamster moves on or continues whatever it was doing before it became alarmed. Hamsters routinely behave like this when they first leave their burrow, stopping briefly at the entry hole to check for strange scents and suspicious sounds.

Face to face with an enemy: Every

hamster's first impulse when confronted with danger is to get back into its burrow. If it's too late for that, it rises up on its haunches and puffs up its cheeks. This may have a deterring effect on smaller opponents, but a dog or another large predator will hardly be impressed. When faced with this kind of enemy, hamsters sometimes play dead. They keel over and lie there motionless, a stratagem that occasionally works.

How Hamsters Move

Hamsters may look clumsy, but when fleeing they run very quickly on straight legs. When they feel ill at ease, as in a strange environment, they advance slowly, belly pressed to the ground. I know one hamster that owes its name to this habit. Because it flattened itself so much during its first venture outside the cage, its owner christened it "Puddle."

In the evening, some hamsters jump up into the air, sometimes as high as 12 inches (30 cm), out of sheer exuberance. Hamsters are also able to swim, though they don't enter the water unless there is no other choice. (Please don't experiment to see whether your hamster can swim!) I have already alluded to the climbing antics of hamsters.

Vocal Utterances

Hamsters don't resort to vocal expression much. They have to find themselves in an extreme situation before they emit sounds that are audible to humans. Some utterances are listed in the table on page 55.

Ability to Learn

Hamsters function primarily on instinct, and their way of life and their behavior are largely determined by inborn patterns of reaction. Still, they sometimes act very intelligently. They investigate every new object and every new situation with curiosity and learn from it. Most hamsters immediately start using any device for exercise they are given.

A young hamster in a posture of subordination toward the older animal.

Beyond this, they get to know their caretaker very well and to tell him or her apart from other people. They do this by identifying and remembering the person's smell and voice. Their reactions to other humans depend on the good or bad experiences they have had with specific people, experiences that are stored in their memory. Thus I know a hamster that regularly disappears into its house when it hears the voice of a neighbor who once stepped on it inadvertently.

Hamsters also remember the places where they have been given tidbits in the past, and when they get hungry they go to those spots to beg for food. But they probably display the greatest inventiveness and persistence in getting precious chunks of food into the nest. A family of my acquaintance told me of a trick their hamster resorted to when trying to cope with a large carrot. After trying to lug the bulky and heavy item and finding it too difficult, it simply kicked it along like a football.

Hamsters rely almost entirely on their noses. They notice and remember only what things smell like, not their appearance, the way we do. Their sense of smell is highly differentiated.

Index

Bold face indicates color photos.

Note of Warning
   There are a few diseases hamsters are subject to that can be transmitted to humans (see page 40). If your hamster shows any sign of illness (see page 42), you should definitely call the veterinarian, and if you are at all worried that your own health might be affected, consult your doctor.
   Some people are allergic to animal hair. If you think you might have such an allergy, ask your doctor before bringing home a hamster.

Perfect for Pet Owners!

PET OWNER'S MANUALS

Over 50 illustrations per book (20 or more color photos), 72-80 pp., paperback.

AFRICAN GRAY PARROTS (3773-1)
AMAZON PARROTS (4035-X)
BANTAMS (3687-5)
BEAGLES (3829-0)
BEEKEEPING (4089-9)
BOXERS (4036-8)
CANARIES (4611-0)
CATS (4442-8)
CHINCHILLAS (4037-6)
CHOW-CHOWS (3952-1)
CICHLIDS (4597-1)
COCKATIELS (4610-2)
COCKATOOS (4159-3)
CONURES (4880-6)
DACHSHUNDS (2888-0)
DALMATIANS (4605-6)
DISCUS FISH (4669-2)
DOBERMAN PINSCHERS (2999-2)
DOGS (4822-9)
DWARF RABBITS (1352-2)
FEEDING AND SHELTERING
  BACKYARD BIRDS (4252-2)
FEEDING AND SHELTERING
  EUROPEAN BIRDS (2858-9)
FERRETS (2976-3)
GERBILS (3725-1)
GERMAN SHEPHERDS (2982-8)
GOLDEN RETRIEVERS (3793-6)
GOLDFISH (2975-5)
GOULDIAN FINCHES (4523-8)
GUINEA PIGS (4612-9)
HAMSTERS (4439-8)
IRISH SETTERS (4663-3)
KEESHONDEN (1560-6)
KILLIFISH (4475-4)
LABRADOR RETRIEVERS (3792-8)
LHASA APSOS (3950-5)
LIZARDS IN THE TERRARIUM (3925-4)
LONGHAIRED CATS (2803-1)
LONG-TAILED PARAKEETS (1351-4)
LORIES AND LORIKEETS (1567-3)
LOVEBIRDS (3726-X)
MACAWS (4768-0)
MICE (2921-6)
MINIATURE PIGS (1356-5)

MUTTS (4126-7)
MYNAHS (3688-3)
PARAKEETS (4437-1)
PARROTS (4823-7)
PERSIAN CATS (4405-3)
PIGEONS (4044-9)
POMERANIANS (4670-6)
PONIES (2856-2)
POODLES (2812-0)
RABBITS (4440-1)
RATS (4535-1)
ROTTWEILERS (4483-5)
SCHNAUZERS (3949-1)
SHAR-PEI (4834-2)
SHEEP (4091-0)
SHETLAND SHEEPDOGS (4264-6)
SHIH TZUS (4524-6)
SIAMESE CATS (4764-8)
SIBERIAN HUSKIES (4265-4)
SNAKES (2813-9)
SPANIELS (2424-9)
TROPICAL FISH (4700-1)
TURTLES (4702-8)
YORKSHIRE TERRIERS (4406-1)
ZEBRA FINCHES (3497-X)

NEW PET HANDBOOKS

Detailed, illustrated profiles (40-60 color photos), 144 pp., paperback.

NEW AQUARIUM FISH HANDBOOK (3682-4)
NEW AUSTRALIAN PARAKEET HANDBOOK (4739-7)
NEW BIRD HANDBOOK (4157-3)
NEW CANARY HANDBOOK (4879-2)
NEW CAT HANDBOOK (2922-4)
NEW COCKATIEL HANDBOOK (4201-8)
NEW DOG HANDBOOK (2857-0)
NEW DUCK HANDBOOK (4088-0)
NEW FINCH HANDBOOK (2859-7)
NEW GOAT HANDBOOK (4090-2)
NEW PARAKEET HANDBOOK (2985-2)
NEW PARROT HANDBOOK (3729-4)
NEW RABBIT HANDBOOK (4202-6)
NEW SALTWATER AQUARIUM
  HANDBOOK (4482-7)
NEW SOFTBILL HANDBOOK (4075-9)

NEW TERRIER HANDBOOK (3951-3)

REFERENCE BOOKS

Comprehensive, lavishly illustrated references (60-300 color photos), 136-176 pp., hardcover & paperback

AQUARIUM FISH (1350-6)
AQUARIUM FISH BREEDING
  (4474-6)
AQUARIUM FISH SURVIVAL
  MANUAL (5686-8)
AQUARIUM PLANTS MANUAL
  (1687-4)
BEST PET NAME BOOK EVER, THE
  (4258-1)
CAT CARE MANUAL (5765-1),
CIVILIZING YOUR PUPPY (4953-5)
COMMUNICATING WITH YOUR
  DOG (4203-4)
COMPLETE BOOK OF
  BUDGERIGARS (6059-8),
COMPLETE BOOK OF CAT CARE,
  (4613-7)
COMPLETE BOOK OF DOG CARE,
  (4158-5)
COMPLETE BOOK OF PARROTS
  (5971-9)
DOG CARE MANUAL (5764-3)
FEEDING YOUR PET BIRD (1521-3)
GOLDFISH AND ORNAMENTAL
  CARP (5634-5)
GUIDE TO A WELL BEHAVED
  CAT (1476-6)
GUIDE TO HOME PET GROOMING
  (4298-0)
HOP TO IT: A Guide to
  Training Your Pet Rabbit
  (4551-3)
HORSE CARE MANUAL (5795-3)
HOW TO TALK TO YOUR
  CAT (1749-8)
HOW TO TEACH YOUR OLD DOG
  NEW TRICKS (4544-0),
LABYRINTH FISH (5635-3),
MACAWS (6073-3),
NONVENOMOUS SNAKES (5632-9),
WATER PLANTS IN THE AQUARIUM
  (3926-2), paperback

Barron's Educational Series, Inc. • 250 Wireless Blvd., Hauppauge, NY 11788
Call toll-free: 1-800-645-3476 • In Canada: Georgetown Book Warehouse
34 Armstrong Ave., Georgetown, Ont. L7G 4R9 • Call toll-free: 1-800-247-7160
ISBN prefix: 0-8120 • Order from your favorite book or pet store

The photos on the Covers:
Front cover: A golden hamster nibbling on a treat.
Inside front cover: Two piebald golden hamsters
with an exercise wheel.
Inside back cover: A boy with his hamster.
Back cover: Cream-colored golden hamster
clambering around on some branches.

English translation © Copyright 1990
by Barron's Educational Series, Inc.

© Copyright 1989 by Gräfe and Unzer
GmbH, Munich, West Germany
The title of the German book is *Hamster*

Translated from the German by Rita and Robert
Kimber

All inquiries should be addressed to:
Barron's Educational Series, Inc.
250 Wireless Boulevard
Hauppauge, New York 11788

Library of Congress Catalog Card No. 90-34407

International Standard Book No. 0-8120-4439-8

**Library of Congress Cataloging-in-Publication
Data**

Frisch, Otto von.
　　[Hamster. English]
　　Hamsters: how to take care of them and
understand them/Otto von Frisch; with photo-
graphs by Karin Skogstad and drawings by
György Jankovics; consulting editor, Matthew M.
Vriends; [translated from the German by Rita and
Robert Kimber].
　　64p. cm.
　　Translation of: Hamster.
　　ISBN 0-8120-4439-8
　　1. Golden hamsters as pets. 2. Hamsters as
pets. I. Title.
SF459.H3F7313 1990
636'.93233—dc20 　　　　　90-34407
　　　　　　　　　　　　　　　　　　CIP

PRINTED IN HONG KONG

3　9927　98